BUBBLE GUM & CHALK DUST

Mary Lou Carney

BUBBLE GUM & CHALK DUST

Prayers and Poems for Teachers

Abingdon Press   Nashville

BUBBLE GUM AND CHALK DUST

Copyright © 1982 by Abingdon

96 97 98 99 00 01 02 03 — 20 19 18 17 16 15 14 13

This book is printed on recycled, acid-free paper.

Library of Congress Cataloging-in-Publication Data

CARNEY, MARY LOU, 1949–
  Bubble gum and chalk dust

ISBN 0-687-03987-8

1. Teaching—Poetry. 2. Religious poetry, American.
I. Title.
PS3553.A7564B8   811'.54   82-4041   AACR2

Illustrated by May Abers

MANUFACTURED IN THE UNITED STATES OF AMERICA

To
my mother,
who
taught me the magic of
prayer

and to
Mrs. Ridpath,
who
taught me the magic of
poetry

1 Dear Lord,
The room is so clean
                    so quiet
                        so empty.

The vacant chairs stare at me
        questioning—as I am—
    the school year that is about to begin.

Bulletin boards flaunt splashes of
        autumn orange, fall brown.
Posters hang precariously by
        masking-tape hands.
Textbooks stand in faultless rows
        shiny new covers free from
            crumpled edges
            bent corners.

All is ready.

All but me, Lord.

I am filled with
        apprehensions
        fears
        unreadiness.
The responsibilities of my undertaking
    are greater than my abilities.

So, help me, Lord.

Give me
    wisdom
        wit
            patience.

Most of all, patience.

2   Dear God,
I made it
   through the first day.

So many faces with
      searching eyes, sullen eyes
      bright blue and smoky brown eyes.

What can I give them—
      addition facts?
      names of oceans?
      parts of speech?

But what else, Lord—
      consistency?
      fairness?
      maybe even love?

O God,
      make my curriculum—
         and me—
            complete.

3   Sandra Tilford.
The name stares up
   from between neat gradebook lines.

I remember the day
   I placed it there—
      carefully forming the S
      making wide, free curves on the T
      wondering if she would be
         flamboyant or shy
         pretty or plain.

The word WITHDRAWN
   fills the emptiness after that name—
      an emptiness that should be filled with
         spelling and math grades
         paragraph and punctuation homework.

WITHDRAWN
But to where, God?
And why?

I feel guilty
      cheated.

I would like to have
      looked into her eyes
      made her laugh.

I would like to have
      touched her
      somehow, God—
         somehow . . .

4 Such big eyes, God.
Jeffrey has such big, attentive eyes.

He seems to
      watch my every move
      accept as gospel my every word.

I don't think I like that, God.
Infallible is uncomfortable for me.

Don't let me
      disillusion him
      disappoint him.

Please.

Make me
      wise as Solomon
      patient as Job.
Make me
      almost as perfect
      as Jeffrey knows I am.

5   O God,
Teach me to cope
  with textbook publishers
   who somehow misplace
   my workbook order

  with inexperienced colleagues
   who flaunt naïve bravado

  with administrators
   who have little empathy.

Teach me to be
  less critical
   more helpful
    Christlike.

Teach me, Lord—
  if I am to teach.

6 It's 10:00 P.M.
  and
 I am tired, dear God,
  but
 the coffee table is covered
  with literature tests
     grammar quizzes
  waiting to be graded.

Tonight I envy people
  who leave their work
   at work.

Tonight I wish my life's profession were
  making detergent boxes or
  sewing the left-leg seam
   of long underwear.

Tonight I resent
  making lesson plans
  marking papers.

Refresh me, Lord.

Remind me that
  worthwhile things are hard.

Get me through
  the next few hours
 with my
  optimism
  dedication
  love of teaching
 still intact.

7   Each morning
        I drive to school
        suffused in the splendor of autumn—
            silver trunks
                toss gold doubloons
            crimson flames
                bend with the breeze.

But too often my mind is on
        that test waiting to be dittoed
        the parent-teacher meeting after school
        ungraded papers that clutter my desk.

O God,
    let my day begin with thoughts of you
    let the spangled beauty of my morning's drive
        awake my numbed senses
        to new reverence and awe.

Help me, Lord,
        to take time
        for tranquility.

8 Today I made a new seating chart
       separating friends
       breaking up cliques.

Now my students sit and glare at me—
       angry
    that I have presumed
    on their private territory
       upset
    that now they must sit by
            Gordon who is *so* fat
            Beverly who *never* talks
            Bob who *knows* he is smart.

Help me win their trust again, Lord.
Let me be
       fair but not vindictive
       strict but not cruel.

Let me discipline with love
    because I know
       it is the only
          effective way.

9 O God,
Today parent conferences begin.

Mothers and fathers
   polite, anxious
   wanting confirmation for
      hopes, expectations.

How can I tell them that
   Robert is overconfident
   Jim seldom applies himself
   Patty has yet to complete a homework
      assignment
   Lori's mouth is as smart as it is active.

Let me remember that
   Robert's grades are good
   Jim is never a discipline problem
   Patty contributes to class discussion
   Lori is always the first one finished.

Let me tread softly
   through other's lives—
      not trample aspirations
         with hardcore test scores
      not damage relationships
         with reported misbehaviors.

O God,
Let me resist the temptation
      to vent my frustrations.
Let me temper truth
      with tact and love.

10 While leafing through last year's planbook
I found the school picture Kim gave me.

I remember
the first day I saw her.
Her eyes were smoldering gray.
She stood determinedly just beyond my reach.

My initial overtures
were met with her
cold, practiced stare.

But I also remember
the first time she allowed her eyes to laugh
the day she stayed after class "just to talk."

O God, I love Kim—
I have loved so many Kims.

Always
our times together
were short—
that's the way it is with
teachers and students
always.

Thank you for Kim, God.

The memory of her slow smile
still reminds me that
barriers can come down
people do need people
and
teachers and students
are really only people, after all.

11 Today we are having
          play tryouts.

Wide-eyed, nervous
    they finger edges
        of new playbooks.

Sally sits reading her lines
    lips moving
        in mute preparation.

Tracy stares at his socks
    deep lines furrow
        his freckled forehead.

JoEllyn laughs too loudly
    talks of past performances
        pretends to be unruffled.

Jealousy roams
    about the room.
Disappointment hovers
    above the rows.

And I sit
        in the seat of judgment—
    pen poised
        above newly dittoed
        evaluation sheets.

Help me, God.
I want
    tryouts, drama, acting
        to be fun for them.

I want to give them again
    the gift of make-believe

the wonder they packed away
  with Barbie dolls
  and Matchbox cars.

Let me communicate
  to every would-be
    actor
    actress
  the value of their being
  the courage of their attempt.

Let my decisions be
  wise
  practical
    and for all these
    fragile, artistic egos
  as painless as possible.

12 Great globs
of the pink wad
mysteriously appear
under desks
on floors
and now on page 488
of my new
Random House Dictionary
stuck between
"joggle" and "joke."

Sour-apple Green
Watermelon Coral
Gruesome Grape

Bubble gum is everywhere.

Like a malignant fungus
it takes over—
opaque bubbles grow
where lips should be.

My room smells
like a stockpile
of moldy fruit.

My questions
are echoed with
pops and snaps and cracks.

Bubble gum.

It seems such a useless thing
to me, God.
But it seems so important
to my students.

O Lord,
I know there are things
in my life
that are as
annoying
irritating
maddening
to you
as bubble gum is
to me.

Show me those things, God.
Make me willing
to become
what you want.

Let me give up all
my bubble gum.

13   Today I follow
a school bus
its red lights winking at me
its chubby yellow body
waddling back and forth
like a mother duck.

Small faces press against the windows
blondes and brunettes
blur behind morning frost.

The bus jerks spasmodically, then stops.
A huge yellow circle blinks
a right-hand turn.

In that instant
of immobility
I come close
to the back of the bus.

The girl in the back seat
who has been brushing her hair
for the last half mile
turns and looks directly at me.

I meet her gaze.

Her eyes are serious, familiar—
borrowed from an old picture or
an Andrew Wyeth painting.

The bus lurches
onto the gravel side road.

As the girl turns around
her copper-colored hair
falls in waves over the back of the seat.

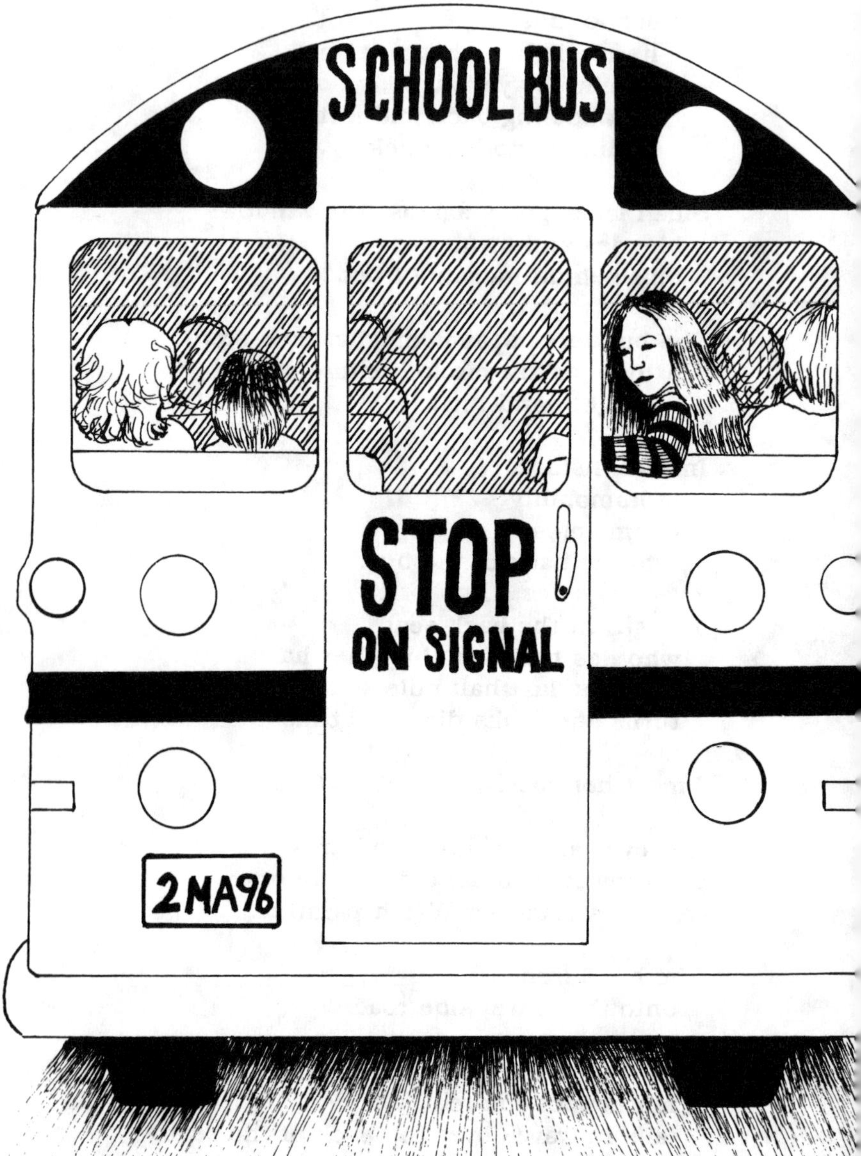
SCHOOL BUS
STOP
ON SIGNAL
2MA96

The bus lumbers ahead, dodging
    mirky country chuckholes.

Suddenly I realize I am blocking traffic.
As I pull ahead
    my mind is on
    the girl.

I wish I had waved
    or smiled.
I wish I had given her
    something other than a stare
    as cold as the smudged windows
        that separated us.

Dear God,
    remove from me the
            apathy
            aloofness
    I reserve for strangers.

Make me aware
    of the small chances
    that come my way.

May I always have
    an open mind
    a listening ear
        an early-morning smile.

14 Every morning
   children crowd near my desk
   vying for attention, recognition.

"Teacher, my tooth came out! See!"
"We might get a dog. A big one."
"Tommy's poking the gerbils."
"Joshua took my pencil, Teacher."
"I didn't take your stupid old pencil.
  This one's mine. It's even got my
  teeth prints on it!"

Many mornings
  I barely listen
  mechanically supplying an
    Uh-huh
    Really?
    Sit down.

That's what I did this morning
  when Mike told me
  his mother was going to the hospital.

Then during seat work
  I heard Mike scuffing the toe of his shoe
    against the tiled floor.
  I saw tears rolling down his chapped cheeks
    splashing onto his flannel shirt.

O God,
  I need to be more sensitive
        more careful.

Help me remember that
  in the midst of teaching
         ministering

you took time
  not only to instruct
  but also to caress
    little children.

Remind me that
  listening to
      exhaustive descriptions of
        Easter vacations
      jokes for the third time
    is as important as listening to
      reading lessons
  looking at
      skinned knees, mosquito bites
      chicken-pox sores, new shoes
    is as important as looking at
      writing assignments.

Let me make time for
  prepared lessons
  meaningful feedback
  enriched activities
  and lots and lots of hugs.

15 Teenagers.

They walk sullenly into the room
    faded denim jackets reeking of reefers
    roach clips proudly displayed in jeans'
       pockets.
Their eyes smolder with misdirected hate
    with abhorrence of "the system."

The air is tinged with
    insinuations
      accusations
        confrontations.

Yet daily I offer myself to them
    offer to them
      excitement of discovery
      joy of learning.
My reason for persistence baffles them.
Its very simplicity clashes with
    their armored defenses.

I teach because I care.

Please, God—
    let them sense that.
In spite of their
    carefully erected barriers
    let them know that I care.

Please, God.

16 Today has been
such an ordinary day.

No bursts of
temper or genius
have broken the methodical pace
of this day.

The trash can is full—
mistaken math
messy English
melodramatic love notes.

The chalkboard is full—
complex sentences
common denominators
class assignments.

But I am empty, Lord.

The very ordinariness of today
has drained me of
enthusiasm
charisma
empathy
creativity.

Fill me, Lord.

Help me remember
that teaching—
and life—
are made up of
ordinary days
patterned by you
into the
extraordinary.

17 On the way to school this morning
    I saw an old man
      hitchhiking.

His face was
   round and
   red with cold.

His coat—
    a relic of Navy days—
   hung awkwardly on his
    stooped shoulders.

He wore a hat
  of black
    with ear muffs
    protruding like
      furry hands.

Timidly
    plaintively
he offered his
   bared thumb.

I looked straight ahead
  and drove on
    turning the heater up to high
    for the car was suddenly cold.

O God—
  I hate living in an age
    when charity is a luxury
      few feel they can afford.
  I hate being one of the many
    who have succumbed
      to headlines and horror stories.

Lord, help me to be
  friendly but not foolhardy
  helpful but not unwary.

May I accept both
  the inherent risks
  the ultimate rewards
    of being Christlike.

18 It's Christmastime, Lord.

Red and green garlands
  border the bulletin boards.
Paper snowflakes
  clutter the windows
    undaunted by afternoon sun.
Swagging Christmas balls
  reflect the faces of children
      expectant
      joyful
      preoccupied.

The Christmas tree is weighted with
  cardboard angels
  paper stars
  glittered circles.

And I must tell them, God—
  tell them how it all began—
    about the manger and baby
          the shepherds and angels
    about your love.

But I must tell them
    gently and simply,
  for skeptics come in all sizes.

It's Christmastime, Lord.

Be with us among the
  snowy-bearded Santas
  foil-bedecked packages
  offerings of children's carols.

Be with us, Lord—
  for without you

Christmas is only clutter and color
as temporary as wrapping paper
as lifeless as needles that drop from
discarded trees.

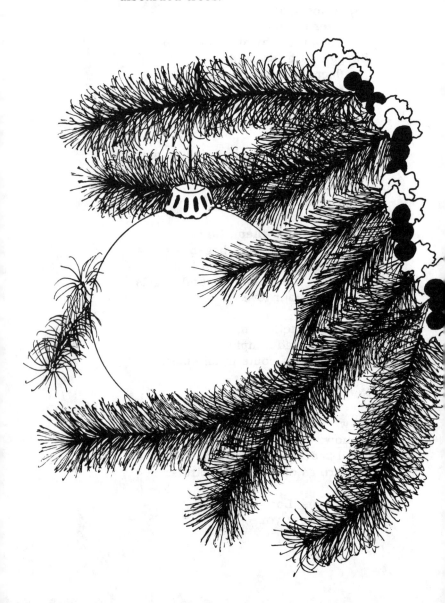

19 Chalk dust
  covers my chalkboard
    with wispy circles
  lurks in the ridges of
    my chalkrail.

Chalk dust
  lingers on my black wool suit
    a tribute to
      my day's industry—
      or clumsiness—
        or both.

Chalk dust
  fills every crevice in my fingers
  saturates each wrinkle in my hands.
I carry it with me like an aura—
  like the inky smell of printers
  or the scrutinizing squint of CPAs.

It is the mark of my profession.

There is comfort in consistency, God—
  in knowing
    the cottony, warm taste
    the silky, illusive feel
    the irksome nasal tickle
  of chalk dust.

It serves its purpose well.

Lord, let me do as much—
  assured each day of
    guidance, help, and
  chalk dust.

20 There is sickness in our school, dear God.
Each day the absence list grows
    longer and l
           o
             n
              g
               e
                r.

My room is strangely empty—
    vacant chairs
    missing faces.

Intermittent silences
    interrupted with coughing
        raspy
        repeated.

Tissues disappear like peppermint drops.

Small cheeks are flushed.
Small eyes are feverish.

I can predict
    whose seats will be empty tomorrow.

O Lord,
    help the sick children
        who lie at home, aching
        who come back to voluminous
                    confusing
                    make-up work.

Help the sick children
    who come to school
        prompted by the fear of falling behind
        prodded by parental unconcern.

Help me
    as I explain the same math fact
      for the thirtieth time
    as I wade through the patchwork pieces
      of make-up work
    as I listen to the never-ending lament
    "I wasn't here when we did that, Teacher."

Give me, God,
    the three things I most need—
      patience
      perseverance
        and good health.

21 Today I received three presents
        an apple
        a drawing
        a poem.

The apple was
        an impromptu gift
        dug from a crumpled brown lunch sack
        packed by an unsuspecting mother.

The drawing was
        a rainbow house
        a smiling child
  and a "strawberry tree"
        the color of cotton candy.

The poem was
        about "Pete the Dog"
          who loved bones and sunshine
          and hardly ever chased a cat.

Three presents, Lord,
  in just one day.

I ate the apple after school.
I taped the drawing to my desk.
The poem looks
  oddly appropriate
  magnet-hung on my
    refrigerator door.

And as I stand here reading
    about Pete one more time
  I dwell on the title
      TO MY TEACHER
  and smile at the realization
    that that's my favorite line.

22 O God,
   I hate conflicts
      arguing
         who's right and who's wrong
      feeling
         anger and hurt and frustration.

   I know things can't always go well.
   I know dissonance
      is not abnormal
      or even unusual.

   I know all that, God—
      but it still bothers me
            still gives me a twinge in the throat
            that could be a sob
            if I were half my age.

   Use conflict in my life, Lord,
      to make my words more kind
            my deeds more noble
            my views more empathetic.

   O God,
      make
         inevitable conflicts
      serve
         divine purposes.

23 I hate the first day in a strange building.
The halls are a maze
  and I the frightened animal
  that must find its way
    not falteringly
    but confidently
  through them.

In the security of my new room
  I sit
    waiting for homeroom students to arrive
      to stare at me with cold—
      or worse yet—
      indifferent eyes.

Shawn is the first.
He half-walks, half-slides to a desk
  just inside the door.
With restless dark eyes he scans the room
  showing equal disinterest in
      worn carpet
      bare bulletin boards
      new teacher.

He is different—
  cerebral palsy?
  mental retardation?

Involuntarily
  I tense
  at his presence.

Other students stream into the room
  breaking around Shawn
    like a swollen, bubbling river
    breaking around a rock in its midst.

In the din of morning amenities
  I hear Shawn's voice.
His speech is slow
  his sounds gutteral—
              almost nonhuman.
His face writhes
  with the task of self-expression.

Pledge of allegiance said
  announcements
    and introductions made
  students gather
    books, gym bags, folders
    and join the surging hallway throng.

I watch Shawn leave.
His right foot stubs into the
  side of his left.
His gait is awkward.
He tugs at his jeans as he walks—
  limp, tug, limp, tug.

It is finally 3:15.

I sit
  with the exhaustion of the unfamiliar.
I look up to see Shawn
  bumping his way
  through the scattered desks.

He looks down at me.
His eyes are flawless black—
  limpid pools of onyx.
He begins
  "Mizz . . . Mizz . . . ."

"Carney," I supply.

He grins.
  "Miz Carney, wel-welcome to our . . . our
  school."

He pivots on his heel.
Contorting his body in accustomed manner
  he makes his way out the door.

I listen to the
  kud-thud, kud-thud
    of his footsteps in the hall.

O God! The things I take for granted—
  the smooth echo of my walk
  the fluent freedom of my talk.

Great Teacher
  who healed the halt and blind and lame
    heal me.

Fill me
  not so much with pity
    as with love.

24 Headlights wind
serpentine
in early morning light.

Snow flits
across the highway
like illusive winter wraithes.

Through the squeaky
ker-swish, ker-swish
of wiper blades
I see icicles
like crystal dragon teeth
hanging from gutterless houses.

The highway throbs
with the hum of a hundred engines
with the rhythmical rotations
of snow tires, radials, recaps.

Thank you, Lord,
for making me a part
of this pre-daylight procession.

Bless those of us
who each day
make our way
to our appointed tasks.
Make us
competent
creative
Christlike.

Especially, Christlike.

25 Report cards
    came out today.

And I gave Jim
    an F, Lord.

A massive red
        F
        that looms ominous
            in the small white square
            shouting silent accusations
                of failure.

I can't reach him, God.

I've tried
    coaching, threatening
    mollifying, encouraging.
I've given him
    extra hints
    extra help.

And still he
    makes no effort
        shows no spark of concern
                no attempt at concentration.

He only grins
    his Cheshire smile
        eyes luminous with mischief
        and just a touch of defiance.

We are at an impasse, Lord.
What shall I do?

How can I accept
    his failure—
        and mine?

26 Sun filters through open-weave curtains
glinting on the burnished chrome of
Ethel's wheelchair.

In the hallway
slippered feet scuff
across polished oak floors
plastic trays rattle
with the sway of the lunch cart.

Ethel's gray hair
slips from her hairnet.
Soft, gossamer strands
frame her face like childish tendrils.

"I myself have always preferred
the gay comedies of Shakespeare.
Why do publishers always anthologize
those gruesome tragedies?
I once had a group of seniors . . ."

As she talks of her teaching days
her eyes take on an intensity of hue
become the dancing blue
of a birthday child or a bride.

Suddenly she shivers.
Still talking
she slips her thin arms
into the green sweater—
misshapen and nubby from many
washings—
that hangs on the back of her chair.
She fumbles with the buttons.

O God,
   help me.

Let me build my memories carefully.
Someday I will have the leisure
   to replay each semester
      of my fragile career.

And when that time comes, Lord,
   let me
      like me—
   lest my declining years
      be filled
   with the frustration
      of regret.

27 O God, I failed today.

At first I didn't notice her
   in the semidarkness of the auditorium.
But as I hurried down the slanted cement aisle
   my quick steps echoing
     in the oppressive stillness
I noticed a shadowy form, a massive lump
   huddled on the edge of the deserted stage.

It was Helen.

She looked up at me
   her moon face dwarfed by her
   too large, too white body.
Her eyes betrayed an innocence and warmth
   that years of name-calling and jeering from
   petite coeds and taut-stomached athletes
     had failed to destroy.

"Hello," she murmured.
And then more cautiously,
   "How are you?"

I nodded and flashed her
   my noncommital smile.
I was in a hurry.

I pushed open the backstage door.
A rush of clamor and conversation
   obliterated the sound of a deep sigh
   that lingered in the
     almost empty auditorium.

Forgive me, Lord.
Slow me down.
Let me take time for
   all the Helens in my life.

28 February snow
  falls outside my classroom window.

Winter winds
  whip and whirl it
    making tiny Christmas-card drifts
    in the corners of the window panes.

My first-graders sit
  restlessly doing seat work.
Anxious eyes steal secret glances
  at the paper-heart-covered door.

Brown bags
  decorated with crudely cut hearts
    of red, pink, white
  line the chalk trays.

Room mothers
  magically appear
    laden with gallons of red punch
    balancing boxes of cupcakes
      sprinkled with chocolate hearts.

The reading table is transformed
  with a red paper cloth and a
      fold-out centerpiece.

Small hands reach up
    expectant, eager
  as I pass out the
    valentine bags.

Stubby fingers feel envelopes
  opening fat ones first

knowing these contain
    flat red suckers
    penny candy
    fistfuls of red-hots.

The room resounds
    with the chaotic chorus of children's voices.
"What does this say, Teacher?"
"Hey, there's no name inside.
    Who's this one from?"
"My name is spelled with two Ts."
"I didn't get a valentine from Jay
    and I gave him my nicest one!"

I open the valentines
    piled on my desk.
Ten of them are identical.
Three contain hankies
    with embroidered hearts in the corners.
One is handmade
    of white lace doilies.
    I LOVE YOU is printed
        in bold red crayon.

Thank you, God,
    for Valentine's Day
    for a day of unabashed
        I Love You.

And someday, Lord,
        when my students experience
        the frustration and wonder of adolescence
    let them remember today
    when love was
        as simple as dime-store valentines
        as tangible as chocolate cupcakes.

29 There is no school today, God.

All night the wind has
   whirled and moaned
      whipping the falling snow
         into mountains of
            angel hair spun with diamonds.

Now I sit snowbound—
   watching the fire spurt geysers of
      purple and orange
   while distant muted voices roar of
      wind and
         snow and
            cold.

O Lord,
   let me never forget your
      beauty
         wonder
            power.

30 It's February, God,
and I notice
an edge to my voice
that was not there
in October.

I notice
a dullness in my students
an apathetic indolence.
Enthusiasm lags
like a tired mule.

Homework is late
or sloppy
or not done at all.

Class discussion is
as barren as the view
from my classroom window.

Dear Lord,
help us all.
Give us
vitality
determination—
and an early spring.

31 He sits—
    the perfect ruffian
  chewing the end of his pencil
  dropping his pen
    often enough to assure him
    constant attention by his
      more domesticated peers.

He sits—
  the incarnation of
    Oliver Twist
    Huckleberry Finn
  poking
    with his mutilated yellow eraser
  the newly assigned pages
    in his reading book.

The end of his nose turns up slightly.
His straight yellow hair hangs in
    uneven sun-streaked strands.

He pushes his pen
    to the edge of his desk.
For an instant it hangs
    suspended
  then hits the carpet with a
    dull, familiar thud.

Our eyes meet—
  mischief dances in his
  determination burns in mine.

"Howard, do your work."

Retrieving his pen
  he bows his head
    in mock obedience.

He pushes his stubby finger
  along the row of black characters.
He pokes his broken nail
  at each word.

The room settles into silence.
Pages turn with gentle swishes
  while I attack anew
  my mountain of ungraded spelling.

But I look up
  just in time to see
    Howard's pen
    roll
      slowly
      deliberately
        to the floor.

O God,
  I can handle
    lunchroom food fights
    playground fist fights
  any open opposition.

But what can I do about Howard?
What can I do about
    his subdued resistance
    his lingering persistence
  in refusing to learn?

Dear Lord, help me
    to be patient
    to give even more
  and *please* help Howard learn
    to keep his pen
      off the floor.

32 Sentence diagrams
cover my chalkboards.

Straight white lines
separate subjects and verbs.
Rockets of compound parts
stand nose to nose.
Prepositional phrases
hang like trapeze artists.

It's all so neat, Lord,
so precise
organized
systematic.

Every piece fits like a
well-cut jigsaw puzzle.

O God,
I wish I could promise
my students
lives as orderly
as well-constructed
as these handpicked
custom-designed sentences
I assign for diagraming.

Let me prepare them, Lord,
for unexpected digressions
unwanted intrusions
baffling confusion—
not only
in sentence diagrams
but also
in life.

33 It's almost spring, Lord.
Smudged snowdrifts cower
   beside thawing highways.
An adventurous crocus
   pokes through ground
   still cold from February frost.

It is time
   for the eternal paradox
   for the blossoming and greening
      of stark brown branches
   for the renewing
      of life long dormant.

It's almost Easter.
And I think of you, Lord,
   in your innocence
                humiliation
                sacrifice.

I think of the
   divine paradox of
      my life
   through
      your death.

And I am humbled
             saddened
   thankful for
      springtime
      a crocus
   and you.

34 As I drove to school this morning
　　it was raining.

Huge drops beat on the windshield
　　forming lucid pools that stared into my car
　　　　until flung by the wipers into oblivion—
　　　　　　with only a squeak
　　　　　　to mourn their passing.

O God,
　　today I feel as though
　　　　my teaching has no real substance
　　　　　　　　　　no more endurance
　　than those raindrops
　　　　that slide off my windshield and
　　　　splash on the hard, dirty pavement.

Help me
　　to overcome these
　　　　feelings of futility.

35 Outside my classroom window
I see a stranded kite.

It flaps
    helpless
yet
    determined.

Bare branches
    tear it with
        indifferent cruelty.

It's been there for days
    purposeless
yet
    captive.

How tragic that
    a yellow kite
        built for soaring
                wind climbing
                current chasing
    languishes in an
    ominous oak.

God,
    sometimes I feel like
    that yellow kite.
The tedium of routine
    traps me.

I want to be
    spontaneous
        creative
            witty.

But instead, I am
  methodical
    repetitious
      maybe even boring.

Lord, make me
  as a canary kite
    soaring
    climbing
    accomplishing.

But keep a firm hand
    on the string, God—
  for I need to know
    and accept my limitations.

That's important
  both for teachers
    and for kites.

36 O God,
  this prayer is for Carolyn
    who sits each day
      trancelike
    who watches me
      with frightened fawn eyes
    who digs her pen
      deep into her pink gum eraser.

She is falling
  farther and
  farther behind.

I find
  each offer of help
    treated as an intrusion
  each proffered assist
    met with stony silence.
For my every overture
    she has an equal—
      almost vehement—
  rebuff.

This prayer is for me too, God.
Because I am tempted
    to leave her alone
    to let her daydream and drift into
      unobtrusive obscurity
    to mark her papers(the few she does)
  and comfort myself
  with the well-known
    "You can't save 'em all."

Dear Lord,
  my pride—
    personal
    professional
  is hurting.

This girl
   thwarts me
   with a stoicism
      dark and determined.

I want to do what's best for Carolyn, God.
I want to give her
   the extra help
                attention
                encouragement
   she needs.

Enable me to
   bury my pride
   redouble my efforts.

Keep me from the comfort of embraced clichés.

Give me
   the persistence
      to offer again—
   the humility
      to risk rejection.

Give me
   the courage to believe
      "All things are possible"
   for Carolyn
      and for me.

37 The clock ticks methodically
in the hallway.

I sit beside my window
mesmerized by early spring sunshine.
Fields shimmer
in shades of variegated lime.
Daffodils have yielded the stage
to an encore of lilacs.

The afternoon stretches before me
tempting me from mundane duties
with promises of woodland walks
uninterrupted solitude.

O God,
the last thing I want to do this afternoon is
diagram sentences
analyze Hawthorne's symbolism
listen to oral book reports.

The bell blares the end of lunch period.
The halls swarm with buzzing adolescents.

Help me, Lord.
I need a cure for
fatigue
boredom—
spring fever.

38 Tissue-paper butterflies
　　with clothespin bodies
　flutter beneath fluorescent fixtures.

Milk-carton flower gardens
　fill the windowsill.
Tiny sprouts of green
　　push through over-watered soil
　　reaching for shafts of spring sun.

My second-graders
　slump in their seats.
Small tousled heads bend over workbooks.
Fingers still dirty from recess kickball
　push fat yellow pencils.

My pointer thuds against the
　colorless spiral chart.
"Words ending in 'nd'
　have both long and short vowel sounds.
Some sounds are spelled
　two ways . . ."

My voice sounds hollow.
I scan upturned faces and
　wonder how reading charts
　can ever compete with
　　thoughts of after-school baseball
　　plans for recess revelry.

Lord, keep me from boredom
　born of repetition.

Remind me that vowel sounds
                consonant blends
                digraphs
      are prerequisites to reading
        newspapers
        novels
          and the Bible.

39 The annual poetry contest
is about to begin, Lord.

Seventh-grade contestants
waiting their turns
sit in rows like
toy-store soldiers.

Stuffed animals
camouflage suits
footed pajamas
cocked baseball hats—
costumes and props
fondled
ruffled
by nervous fingers.

Approaching the mike
they abandon their identities—
become
Lil' Orphan Annie washing cups
Ogden Nash's Isabel "eating a bear up"
an alligator with a sore tooth
a surviving veteran, sad and aloof.

Such exuberance!
Such talent!

How can I channel it, God?
How can I keep alive their
creativity
spontaneity
while teaching the necessary
conformity
moderation?

Help me to capitalize
   on their energy
      their enthusiasm.

Make my teaching
   as
      imaginative
      uninhibited
   as
      my poetry students
      are today.

40 The baseball diamond glistens
    with sprinklings of
        springtime gold.

While other children
    swing and slide and play
        Red Rover
    Amy makes her way
        gingerly through
          the dewy grasses
        carefully choosing
          the largest of the flowers.

As she turns and
        runs back toward the playground
    her chubby hand can scarcely hold them all.
They tumble free
    only to be retrieved and
          shoved again
    into her small fist.

As she nears me she slows her pace.
With sparkling blue eyes
    she presents to me the
        fuzzy, crushed blossoms.

O God,
    grant me again
    the simplicity of childhood.
Give me
    the generosity
        of unrequited giving
    the diligence
        of unrewarded work
    and the innocence
        of dandelion bouquets.

41 There was another fight at school today, God.

As I came down the steps from the library
  I saw the small circle of gawkers
    standing shoulder to shoulder
    tense and expectant.
  I heard the sound of books and folders
    being flung to the floor.

Edging my way through the crowd
  I could hear the name-calling—
    boyish voices shrill and unconvincing
    in their shouted insults.
  I could see the pushing—
    each combatant reluctant yet eager
    buoyed up by the cheers of his peers.

Before I could reach them
  the larger boy threw a punch.
His knuckles made a wet smacking sound
  as they landed firmly
  on the other boy's cheek.

Both went down in a tumble of
  denim and plaid
    tennis shoes kicking wildly
    bare arms flailing blindly.

O God,
  I hate these fistfights
    the false bravado
        needless pain.

Adolescents struggle with the
    fervor of confused conviction—

certain that might is right
        that the test of manhood is the
      ability to inflict physical pain.

How can I teach them, God, that
  tolerance is strength
  compromise is courage?

Help me, Lord.
Give me patience, wisdom, tolerance
  lest in my zeal to reform
    I find myself
      like my students
    resorting to force.

42 O God,
    I'm changing schools
      again
        and today I had to say good-bye
    to Jackie.

"We'll keep in touch,"
    she said—
    as I packed
      literature anthologies
      manila folders
        and just a few dreams.

"Sure,"
    I said—
    as I scattered
      red markers and blue pens
      among boxes of battered paperbacks.

But the conversation was familiar—
    other people
    other places
    other times—
      same words.

We stood in the empty room.
Bulletin boards the color of
      dead oak leaves
      stared at us.
Our voices echoed.
Our words were too loud.

"See you soon," she said.
I forced a smile.
"Real soon," I replied.

But the good-byes
    that eluded our lips
        found refuge in our eyes.
With those only
    we said good-bye.

As she walked away
    she yelled over her shoulder.
"Call me sometime!"
"Sure!" I answered
    waving my arm.

I waved longer than was necessary.

Even after she turned the corner
    I could hear the sound of her steps
        clattering like the rocks I used to throw
        on the tattered tin roof of the barn.

Dear God,
    stay close to me
        for I am frightened
            confused
                and just a little angry.

Remind me that
    my times are in your hand.
Let me accept your will
    even when it means saying good-bye to
        accustomed surroundings
        completed planbooks
        familiar anthologies
            and to Jackie.

43 Carefully I count crumpled permission slips.
Kindergartners cluster nearby
  excited yet awed
  by the imminence of
    THE FIELD TRIP.

Chaperones board the bus
  strangely serious
    amid the bubbling bustle of five-year-olds.

"Who's gonna drive the bus?"
"How far to the zoo?"
"When do we eat?"
"Don't sit on my sandwich!"
"Teacher, tie my shoe."

Sandy's schoolday braids today boast
  blue satin bows.
    "For the field trip, Teacher.
      Ain't they nice?"

Tiny tousled heads
  stare out school bus windows
    at the uncharted wonders
    of Highway 2.

O God,
  make me again
    like a little child.
Let me experience the
  fascination of anticipation.
Fill me with an enthusiasm
  born of expectation

fed by appreciation of
   freshly mown hayfields
   slithering bright King snakes
   and only slightly squashed
   peanut butter-and-jelly sandwiches.

44 On a genuine
imitation wood base
my classroom globe sits.

Countries and continents
of faded pastels
swim in a too-blue ocean.

With the push of a finger
the world whirls by—
Mexico, Africa, Asia.

O God,
the world is so big—
yet year after year I find myself
putting up the same bulletin boards
teaching the same spelling lists.

O God,
the world is so big—
and my classroom is so small.
Keep me from smallness, Lord.

Let me never equate
size or salary
with importance.

And remind me that
Nazareth, too,
was a small
small
place.

45 This week it is my turn
  for playground duty
 to stand sentry on the cement
   during morning recess.

Children dart across
  dark patches of asphalt
    racing for monkey bars and swings.

Later at lunch
  they will compare callouses
  boast of one-handed heights
    and airborne feats.

Playground balls
   red and rubbery
  bounce on cracked sidewalks
    with unrhythmical thuds
  roll across stubby grass
    kicked by tattered tennis shoes.

And above the prattle of play
  sound the inevitable conflicts
                    complaints.

"Hey, it's mine!"
"I wanna turn at bat!"
"Teacher, Tommy—he be messin' wif' people!"

I respond with stock replies
        with admonitions
    as old as blackboards
    as predictable as December flu.

"Really now, can't we get along?"
"You can't always have things your way."
"Treat other people the way you want to be
    treated."

The trill of my silver whistle
    signals the end of recess.
Strands of hair
    stick to sweaty foreheads
  as children shuffle from play
          form tittering lines
          file into the cool darkness
          of carpeted corridors.

Dear Lord,
  let me remember the advice
  I glibly give my students.
Let me realize the value of compromise
         the importance of peace
  not only on the playground
  but in my life, as well.

46 The annual autograph party
is being held after school today.

Yearbooks pass across cafeteria tables.
Pens scrawl memories
across glossy prints of
homecoming
cross-country
prom.

Voices mingle in cries of
"Sign mine."
"You *didn't* write *that!*"
"What an awful picture of me."

Years later
these yearbooks
will be dusted and opened
to show wide-eyed children
mommy was a cheerleader
daddy was all-conference champ.

Years later
these yearbooks
will be the Aladdin's lamp of
forgotten faces
lost laughter
teachers with tired eyes.

In the years to come, God,
let my students remember me.
Let me be more than
one more faculty member
staring out from pages of black and gray.

Please Lord,
  let me be remembered
  lest my life's work
    be no more than
    red ink and
    redundancy.

47 Thank you, God, for
  lumpy cornbread muffins
    still warm from home-ec ovens
  half-wilted bouquets of
    September marigolds, April lilacs
  surprise birthday parties featuring
    homemade cakes with too many candles
  Christmas perfumes in
    battered boxes.

Thank you, God, for
  serious questions
  smiles of success
  chances to share love.

Thank you, God, for
  this tiring, rewarding
  frustrating, incomparable
    job of teaching.

48 I don't like Larry, God.
I have tried and tried
  but I really
    don't like Larry.

He darts squirrel-like around the room.
His pencil "accidentally" breaks
  at least three times an hour
  and his trip to the pencil sharpener
    is invariably marred by
      a kicked desk
      a trampled book
      a pulled pigtail.

He is a menagerie of
  guttural grunts
  cringing caterwauls.

His work is a combination
  of camouflauge and catastrophe
  of disjointed scrawlings with
    anemic pens
    dull pencils.

What can I do, God?
Small resentments
     annoyances
  have built an imposing wall
between Larry and me.

In the midst of my martyrdom,
  wondering how anyone
  could love someone so unlovable as Larry
I am reminded of your love for me
         your death for me
  when I am so unlovable.

Help me, Lord.
Remind me often of my own immaturity
                    my own incompetence
            in your eyes.

Keep me from the desire
    to force each student
    to fit my model.

And as for Larry, dear God,
    let me accept the challenge
        to change
            and also to love.

49 Today I received a letter from Wes.
The pale-blue envelope
    was postmarked Fort Bragg, North Carolina.
It has been almost a year
    since he joined the Army
    anxious to
        "blow this one-horse town."
But his letter was filled with
    a nostalgia born of
    distance and homesickness.

Zacek stopped by to see me when
    he was home for spring break.
He plays rugby for Purdue University.
He seems taller, more serious.
He talked of computers and fraternities
                politics and GPAs.

Dawn called to tell me
        she got a B in freshman composition
    and has decided to go into
        criminal law.

Mark sent me a graduation announcement.
He is valedictorian of his college class.

Karen Sue sent me a wedding invitation.

O God,
    my former students have grown up.

While I was busy
        grading other papers
        preparing more lectures
    my students
        became adults.

I'm glad, Lord,
   that some of them keep in touch
      including me in their new maturity.

It's good to know
   that students can grow
      into friends.

50 The school is engulfed
in awesome silence.

No library-bound students
clatter through the halls.
No squeak of clarinet, no thud of timpani
issue from the band room.
No sound of filmstrip or cassette
is heard through corkboard walls.
No clang and crash of home-ec pots and pans
drift through closed doors.

Every student in
every room is taking a
final exam.

Pencils scratch across grosgrain paper
figuring fractions
shading-in circles
writing the right vocabulary word.

This is the final accounting—
the moment that differentiates between
the studious and the unstudied
the industrious and the daydreamer.

O God,
help these students as they
try frantically to remember
the right phrase
the exact fact.

May I evaluate
carefully, fairly—
aware that
someday I too
will have a final accounting.

Let me learn my lessons well, Lord,
lest I am found lacking
with no chance to repeat lessons
                    rectify errors
or raise my final score.

51 In the back corner of my room
    perched atop a gray metal filing cabinet
is a spider plant.

Sprawling brown leaves
  hang listlessly over the sides
    of the yellow plastic pot.
The dirt is dry and hard
  cratered with tiny crevices
  strewn with dead leaves.

I forgot to water it, God.

It seemed like such a small omission
  in the scurry of everyday teaching.

But my spider plant is dead.

And as I stand here
  pounding the sides of the yellow pot
  watching the caked earth
    fall into the trash can
  I wonder
    how many of my omissions—
      a compliment unspoken
      a smile not given
      some small gesture left undone—
  will lead to
    uncalculated consequences.

Help me, God,
  to tend well
    the lives entrusted to my care.
Let me keep them from
  the drought of neglect.

Let my omissions not create
lives as dry as this dirt
spirits as inert as
this dead spider plant.

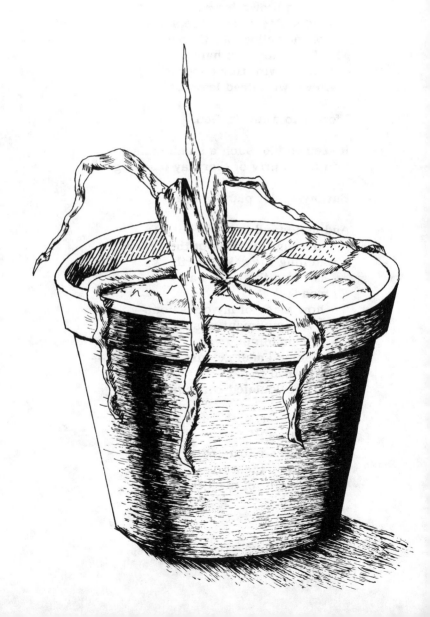

52 Dear Lord,
    the room looks so empty
      block walls with
        oh-so-straight mortar joints
      empty bulletin boards
      assorted cardboard boxes filled with
        fading dittoes
        paper snowflakes
        dog-eared teacher's manuals.
The halls are empty and dark.
Other teachers have gone
  to play golf or tennis or
  to just celebrate
    now that the school year is over.

But I wanted to stay and thank you, Lord.
It's been a busy year—and a good one.

Thanks for giving me patience
      with the slow learners
      with the class clown.
Thanks for giving me a sense of humor
      when I found the hermit crab
      buried among the test papers.
Thanks for giving me
      enough wisdom to teach the classics
      enough energy to direct the musical.
Thanks for giving me
      opportunities for after-school talks
      about the things that really matter.

Thanks for trusting me
  enough to let me teach.

Oh, yes—and thanks
  for summer vacations.